REDMOUTH

Redmouth

Claire Wahmanholm

TINDERBOX
EDITIONS

ISBN: 978-1-943981-14-4

Tinderbox Editions
Molly Sutton Kiefer, Publisher and Editor
Red Wing, Minnesota
tinderboxeditions@gmail.com
www.tinderboxeditions.org

Cover design by Nikkita Cohoon
Cover photograph, "Saga XI" by Inka & Niclas
Interior design by Nikkita Cohoon
Author photo by Daniel Lupton

CONTENTS

REDMOUTH

NOCTURNE

Nights exist, nightshade exists
the dark side, the cloak of namelessness exists
Inger Christensen

Night and nightshade, yes, but also
            the night-blooming Cereus, itself
a cloak of nameless fragrance,
            its face an hours-long brightness
in the desert, crumpling under morning's
            fist—yes, the night-bloomers
and also the nightingale, night-
            song, night-dew, the nightside
of the heart as if it were a moon,
            the privacy, how lush,
how much its hushedness is a cloak
            against the wind of terror, which drives
the names of all our favorite things
            to the edge of the cliff—so yes,
the asylum of namelessness exists, and also
            rest, and the turning from rest
into nothingness, the kind you'd never know
            was happening, the eye within which
you have always been slowly spinning.

ELEGY WHERE MY SORROW APPEARS AS AN UNDISCOVERED LAND

> *Bear violets now, you bramble-bushes and thorntrees,*
> *Let the world turn cross-natured, since Daphnis dies.*
> *Let the prickly juniper bloom with soft narcissus,*
> *The pine be weighed with pears. Let the stag hunt the hounds,*
> *Let the nightingale attend to the screech-owl's cries.*
>   Theocritus

I row across five oceans to reach its bay,
or I wake up one morning to find myself embalmed

in its bees and flowers, or I drag myself through
its gorse hedge mazes. The garden grass

is tender and wet. The gorse does not hurt.
The dragging feels like falling asleep—each thorn draws

a drop of ether through the surface of my skin
until I am a lake. I float on myself for a long time,

expecting to drown but not drowning. Expecting
someone else to arrive. This land goes on and on

in every direction. There is no center, only violet clouds,
or clouds in the shape of beasts I have never seen,

or beasts whose teeth are nightingale feathers.
When I say this land needs a queen, I mean

I could stay here forever. If this dream will one day
strangle me sleeping in its vines, I will

not struggle. Within its evergreen map I will
sleep, a dull and sapless leaf.

THE NEXT WORLD

Let wolves run away from sheep
       Virgil

This was grief's promise—that this next world
would be lamb-lioned, a reversing of the hemispheres.

That I would find myself blinking beneath a eucalyptus sky,
wringing a primrose ocean from my hair
while grief stroked my back, murmuring lie after lie.

But I staggered from the cave and found the same blue
storm clouds, the same trees that bled what they always bled.
The wind felt the same on my mouth. Eras passed.

Once I thought I saw a long-tongued wolf panting
through a pasture. Once I thought I saw a golden apple,
but I am no fool. I know those apples are cast from hunger.

And though it ambles toward me, I will not pat
the terrible sheep with wolf-blood in its wool.

Muses, sing for a herdsman, sing me your song.

Thyrsis from Etna asks you. Listen to his voice.

Where were you, Nymphs, when Daphnis came to **grief**?
What distant valley or mountain gave you delight?
You could **not** be found beside Anapus, the **great river,**
Nor by the water of Acis, nor on Etna's height.

Muses, sing for a herdsman, sing me your song.

Jackals and wolves howled their lament for Daphnis.
The lion wept in **its** forest-bound retreat.
Many the cattle that watched about him dying,
The bulls and cows and calves couched at his feet.

Muses, sing for a herdsman, sing me your song.

Hermes came from the **mountain,** said to him, "Daphnis,
Tell me what passion hurts you. Who is to blame?"
The cowherds, shepherds and goatherds gathered round him,
"Tell us your trouble," they asked. Old Priapus came.

Muses, sing for a herdsman, sing me your song.

"Daphnis," he said, "an unhappy girl goes searching
Each glade and spring for the one on whom she dotes.
Are you her lover, incompetent, feeble-hearted?
You should change your cattle and take a flock of goats;
You are no better than a goatherd, watching and pining
While the billy does his work and the nanny bleats.

Muses, sing for a herdsman, sing me your song.
"In tears you watch the girls, you hear their laughter;
Poor hobbledehoy, you long to join their dance."

But the cowherd drew near the limit of his passion,
Deaf to taunts, absorbed in a **bitter** trance.

Muses, sing for a herdsman, repeat your **song**.

Next came Cypris, her smile sweet and **empty**;
Her heart was **heavy**, her cheerfulness a pretence.
"You boasted you were a match for Love in wrestling;
You lie there **overthrown** for your offence."

Muses, sing for a herdsman, repeat your song.

Daphnis answered her, "Tormenting Cypris,
Hateful to all men, goddess of jealous pride,
Do you think my last sun is sinking? Even in Hades
Daphnis will be the **thorn in** Love's sleek side.

Muses, sing for a herdsman, repeat **your** song.

"They say that a certain cowherd…Hurry to Ida,
Anchises lies there on a bed of galingale;
The oaks will screen you, the humming bees tell no tale.

Muses, sing for a herdsman, repeat your song.

"Adonis the shepherd-boy needs to take a lover.
He hunts the hare and chases all kinds of prey.
Go set yourself before Diomede, and tell him
'Daphnis paid for his boldness. You too must pay.'

Muses, sing for a herdsman, repeat your song.
"Goodbye, you wolves and jackals, you skulking b**ear**s.
The forest-glades and thickets where you hide
Shall never see me again. Goodbye Arethusa,
Goodbye, you streams that pour down Etna's side.

Here Daphnis fed his cattle, here he watered them:
Remember him in the place where he lived and died.

Muses, sing for a herdsman, repeat your song.

"O Pan, are you ranging **the long hills** of Lycaeus
Or the heights of Maenalus? Leave your ground and come
To Sicily. Leave Helice's peak and the mountain,
Cherished by the gods, where Arcas has his tomb.

Goodbye to the herdsman, Muses, goodbye to the song.

"Come, master, and take this pipe of mine, sweet-smelling.
Fastened with wax, the lip-piece delicately bound.
Love **drags me into** the **darkness** where no songs sound.

Goodbye to the herdsman, Muses, goodbye to the song.

"Bear violets now, you bramble-bushes and thorntrees,
Let the world turn cross-natured, since Daphnis dies.
Let the prickly juniper bloom with soft narcissus,
The pine be weighed with pears. Let the stag hunt the hounds,
Let the nightingale attend to the screech-owl's cries."

Goodbye to the herdsman, Muses, goodbye to **the song**.

He said nothing more. Aphrodite **struggled** to raise him,
But the thread allowed by the Fates had run **to its end.**
Daphnis drew near the water and the current took him,
Unhappy child of the Muses, the Nymphs' lost friend.

Goodbye to the herdsman, Muses, **goodbye** to the song.

BEAST & MASTER

To stop myself from choking on the tongue of my loneliness,

I carried a groan in my throat. Mostly it sat silent, but at night

I untethered it note by note. It pillared above me in the dark,

curling into the shape of a dog, a horse, a goat. It made a moat around me

with its moaning. Beneath the heavy trees I slept and feared no predators.

Each morning I made myself into a boat, my arms' oars laboring

through thick waters.
                          One by one I pulled more from my throat

and named them after my most familiar nightmares. I called one

Fire-in-the-Barren-Orchard. I called another Rising Water.

And one Suffocating-in-Slow-Motion. I carried them like daughters.

One day I put a blade to my throat and begged the groans to stop

but they only became coyotes howling at the dome of my skull.

Thereafter we lived like beast and master. When they ran I ran

after them faster. When I lay at their feet they called me sweet names.

PRESERVE

The forest is long and songless.
All the animal calls have been cut
down. They lie in stacks along the path:
songbird bindle, parcel of fox throats,
packet of bobcat hollers. I try to recall them
but they won't come. My own calls
are hollow and numb in my neck,
and what would come to that kind of call?

The forest is tall and all the trees hum
with some new hum I can't name.
It pins me through the lungs. The air ambers
around my arms as I swing them.

I am trying to imagine the bird will re-spool,
the fox re-fur and return, panting, to my hands.
But I am already a specimen. Cotton puffs
from my ears like pinfeathers. In my chest,
a tingling like my lungs are falling asleep.
Whatever was deep in me is rising to the surface,
pressing its face against my unblinking eyes.

CHILDREN ARRIVE IN THE LAND
I THOUGHT I WAS ALONE IN

One dusk I hear them out in the fields,
their voices skittering through the pasturage like mice
or the shadows of hawks.
                    At dawn I see the children
flashing among the stands of young birches,
their arms thin as rib-bones, their faces wind-reckless.

How did they arrive in this nettled world
where an even rougher wind scrapes a rough sky
redder every dusk?
               However they came, they soon become
bee-stung and brave. They howl like foxes, wild
at the mouth with their own pitch. The wind sends curtains
of pollen billowing across their lips, sends summer
slipping away in a warble of vowels. The future moans
like flies from an unseen source, worse for its furry vagueness.

I don't tell the children this. I let them find the body
and poke it with their sticks.
                   When they startle real foxes
from their dens and bend toward their redness, I let them.
I do not tell them how sharp and how deep
the future can come. I do not say how lonesome.

MY LIFE AS A NIGHTJAR

Dear nightjar,

dear hunkered-down
hunger:

teach me
(born un-swan,

born a squat goat-
sucker)

crypticity,

the art of lying low-
hearted,
splay-bodied,

hidden
in bracken.

Sing your churr
into the heath
of my ear.

Into my moth-mouth,
feed me dusk.

Your shadow-
less flight,
the crepuscular
signature
of your feather

is one
I am suited for.

As everything tumbles
softly
into smaller

and smaller things,

your whip-poor-will torpor
is indivisible.

My heart is already tumbling
into rock,
into acorn,
a thorn.

I am already
lorn.

I am already
nearly not here.

DEHISCENCE

The world buckled.

The children awoke and I lay them back down, belly up.
I lay the turnips back down, the fretful tulips.
I covered them again in dirt.

When I stood outside and faced west, I felt salt
from the dead ocean gust toward me like gnats or rain.

When the earth lurched again, the garden broke open
for good. Bed after bed spat out its bulbs;
the children spat out their teeth into their hands.
They wouldn't be resown.

I used to watch for deer, but they have disappeared.
When I close my eyes I can see them
licking the coats of their fawns, anchoring
their spots to their fur to their bodies to the forest floor.

The children's hair lies dewy on the hillocks of their heads
until shreds like cornsilk come off in the breeze.

All night I collect flowers from beneath the bare trees.

THE VALLEY

The mountains have unraveled into sand.

In small enough pieces, everything returns
to its first softness: a silk, a wind.

The mouse is soft in the snake's mouth.
The snake is soft as a ripple through the pond,
which used to rest in the mouth of the mountain.

My stomach is red knots in a red curtain.
Softly as a grain rolling in an anthill, one knot
is starting to untie itself. In the mirror I watch
my mouth redden at the margins like a poisoned pond.

A condor's wings cast smoke over its waters.
The forest shivers spores from its leaves.
Sometimes a shadow clots my lungs, breaking
my breaths into smaller and smaller ones.

I do not feel my red stomach, my red mouth,
the smoke, the spores, the shadows.

The softness of it all is awful, like watching
an earthquake on mute. As if the sound of it
could catch on the air and steady the earth.

The soles of my feet are clouds that rain me
numbly into the long grass until the valley is a bowl
of sunset-colored water, deepening and deepening.

THE LAVENDER FOREST

As much dart as dark, quickness as quiet.
Nests of bird bonelets. Nests of crushed zeroes
some snake has sucked dry

the same way the air has sucked
the blood from the leaves and bark
of the forest. Dust.

Everything is so dry it burns my eyes
to look. The brook has vaporized.
Its soft mud bed is soft powder.

Behind the trees, each inch of sky
is tender, lilac-lit. Each finger of clouds
is a matchstick struck.

The animals paw at the hot velvet
of their ears. In the lavender forest,
I learn to touch my own face

very lightly, like ash on a skin of snow,
like a snowflake on the skin
of a freezing lake.

At night, I dream of water. I dream
I am a frog in a human coat. Someday
I will molt from my name and eat it,
crushing that sorrow gently in my jaws.

THYRSIS

That pinetree by the spring and **your touch** on the pipe:
Both whisper **a** music to draw the listener in
With its **sweetness**, goatherd**. Only** Pan plays sweeter.
If he chooses the horned goat, you shall take the she-goat
For your prize. If he takes the she-goat, the kid shall be yours.
It tastes delicious, **the** flesh of an **unmilked** kid.

GOATHERD

Your **song is sweeter**, shepherd**,** than **the waternoise**
Made by the stream **tumbling from the rocky spout.**
If the Muses claim the ewe as a gift, you shall have
The plump pet lamb. If they want the plump pet lamb
You shall take the sheep, and be second only to them.

THYRSIS

Sit down **no**w, goatherd. (think the Nymphs had asked you)
And play your pipe, here where the hillside steepens
And **tamarisks grow** on the slope. I will watch your goats.

GOATHERD

There must be no piping at midday, shepherd, **none:**
We are scared of Pan. Now is the time when he rests
Tired out from the morning's hunting. He can turn nasty,
Tilting his nose at us, quick to take offence.
But, Thyrsis, **you have** composed 'The Passion of Daphnis'
And have **made yourself a** master of herdmen's song.
Let's sit underneath this elm, with the **glade** before us**:**
There Priapus stands, there water spreads and **gush**es
By the oaks and the shepherds' bench set into the hill.
If you sing as you did in the match with Libyan Chromis

I will let you have a goat that can suckle twins
And fill two pails besides, to be milked three times;
And will give you a deep, two-handled cup, new-made,
Washed in fresh wax, still fragrant from the knife.
About the lip of the cup an ivy pattern
Is carved, with golden points among the leaves:
A fluent tendril flaunting its yellow bloom.
Beneath is a woman's figure, delicately worked:
She is robed and wears a circlet to keep her hair.
On either side of her stand two bearded suitors
Arguing their claim. But she takes no notice,
Looks smilingly at one man, or so it appears,
Then at the other; while, hollow-eyed with love,
They struggle against her kindly indifference.
Beside these is carved an aged fisherman.
On a jutting rock. He strains at the very edge
Of his strength to draw in a net with its heavy catch.
You can see the effort bunching in each tense limb
And in his neck as he gives himself to the task.
He has white hair, but his strength is supple and fresh.
A little distance from the old man's sea-labour
There is a vineyard hung with darkening clusters.
A small boy perches on a dry stone wall to guard them.
Two foxes shadow him. One sneaks along the rows
For plunder; another has fixed her tricky eye
On the quarter-loaf the boy keeps for his breakfast
And will not let him alone till she has snatched it.
Blithely intent, he shapes a cage for a cricket
From asphodel stalks and rushes. The bag with his food
Is forgotten; so are the vines. The toy absorbs him.
The base of the cup is overspread with acanthus.
A goatherd's treasure! It is too fine a thing.
I paid the Calydna ferryman a good price for it,
A goat, a large cheese made of the best milk.
It felt too precious to drink from; I put it away

Unused. But how cheerfully I would part with it
For **that** beautiful **elegy.** Do you think I mock you?
No holding back! **You** cannot take your song with you
In the end. Hades **and forgetfulness are the same.**

NATIVITY, REDSHIFT

Once there was space inside of you:
a red cobweb of moonlets, a satellite
spinning in a rocky crèche. Balsam firs
in the foreground. Cold coins in the snow
like stars. This land is one you are lost in.
You may or may not be dreaming. You may
or may not know you are dreaming. You have
found yourself in the middle of a world
that keeps pulling away from you. Here—
the road uncoils its crests and troughs,
the sea billow levels into a line. The air
will thin and thin and thin and whatever
is behind the balsams will open itself
to let you in.

ON MAKING ONE'S PASSAGE
IN THE DARK

Making your way through the woods at night,

                            your heart sometimes splits

to follow two forks of a dark path.

                 Each stretches its nerves toward the other

until the forest fills with the sound of their reaching.

                         The dark rolls

of birchbark flutter with it.

              The dark throats of bats swallow the path

until your hearts twitch and spook into a run,

                   calling for each other,

fumbling for a clearing where there is none.

                  Their fibers cobweb the woods

as they move together and apart.

                One heart harvests bark glowing with rot

and foxfire.

        The other imagines it is a match moving through a warm field

of hay.

      All night they push together and away, the foxfire heart pulsing

with a cold light,

      the hay heart pining after sparks.

FALLOW

Follow the field into its summer, into its faun-colored heat,
its tall, feathery yarrow.
        Look down at the untilled clouds breathing
in the pond, whose water is so shallow and shadowless it's hot.
Harrows withdraw to the horizon, dragging wide, weeded furrows
for you to lay your body in.
        What a bad year it's been. What a slow
wallow of a season.
        Lay it down. Lay it down and wait
for the cross-plough's hatch and scatter. Remember the fish pond
and its clouds, its stalks of swamp rose mallow, the wide-leafed sallows.
Remember the hollow smell of waiting.
        Soon, haying. But not until
your teeth are tilled, are tilth. Not until the rhizomes of your bones
have been pulled and killed.
        Lie low and let the swallows pick you clean.
When the future arrives it will rise willow-green from your yellow eyes.

REDMOUTH

No sheltered world
    Tomas Tranströmer

Among the other flowers in the garden, your mouth
is a red lily gaping toward the sound of war,

Eris, terror. Among the other mouths,
your mouth is the redder. You are a symptom,

or you are an omen. You are sure that this sickness
is one you were born with. You have failed

to thrive in this world that turns its beauty
against you, whose birds and canyons and conifers

are trying to devour you despite how small
you are trying to seem. But you can be smaller.

You can be a stone, a pebble, a grain.
You can lie in the river and watch the rain bulleting

the water above your face. Cough your redness
into your hand, which is suddenly made of air.

This land is an atlas in which you no longer appear.

BREACH

sometimes an anchor snags in a green meadow,
sometimes a curving keel may graze the vines
Ovid

Sometimes you wake to find your pasture changed.

Sometimes you wake a free creature and shake

your horselimbs. Sometimes your future seems

a heavy thing to float in. You are a flight animal

but some mornings you limp. Some mornings teem

with fish you cannot digest with your horse belly.

You have keen horse eyes but underwater the colors

are dim and the depths are full of teeth you cannot

outswim.   One morning you wake to a punctured lung

and several broken ribs. *This is no longer your orchard,*

sigh your lungs. This is no longer your nest of grass.

An anchor snags on your broken chest. A keel carves

your back. You wish you were made for this,

that you could wake to find your posture changed,

that your body could thin and blend with the waterline.

You dream until the pounding of your hooves breaks

the night's ground into
                                another morning where you

have not yet drowned. You know these mornings

are running out—each sun rises more dimly, sprouts

less freely from the water, wavers for just an hour

over the waves before surrendering. You are soon to be

un-creatured, unsutured from your pasture blade by blade.

Why aren't you running. Why aren't you afraid.

REQUIEM

You fall through ballrooms of bare water,

through blossoms of salt gardens. You name

the colors as they deepen: first blueness,

second blueness, first cyan, second cyan,

then cerulean, Persian, ultramarine, then

sapphire, zaffre. Your voice is no longer

a voice but a small underwater explosion—

bubbles of coral in your throat, in the kelp

of your hair.
                But you had been turning to stone

long before you fell. All night, on land,

you had been fossilizing. All day, walking

through sun fields, you had not felt

the florets of grasses between your fingers,

had not watched your own hands crush them

into pebbles, into a trail you would not follow

home. Now, time is stacking body-shaped

spaces above you as you fall, and though

it will take days to reach the floor, you are falling

heavily. If your eyes were not empty already,

you would see for miles through the path

your face is making in the water.

The cool shadows of night had scarcely gone
Away from the morning sky, just at the time
When the dew on the tender grass most pleases the flock,
When, leaning on his elegant olive-staff,
Damon began his song:
                              "Arise, O star
That greets the brightening day, while I lament
Because my sworn love Nysa has deceived me;
Although no help has come for me from them,
I call on the gods to witness as I die.
        My flute, begin to play Maenalus' song.
There's music in the groves that grow upon
The sides of Mount Maenalus, music of Pan,
Who first called music forth from silent reeds,
The songs of shepherds telling of their loves.
        My flute, begin to play Maenalus' song.
Nysa given to Mopsus! What is it that
Lovers can hope for? Griffins and mares will mate,
And in the next age the timid doe will come
Down to the stream to drink along with dogs.
        My flute, begin to play Maenalus' song.
Let them light up the torches, Mopsus, they
Are bringing you your bride. The Evening Star
Is rising for you now from behind the mountain.
        My flute, begin to play Maenalus' song.
That she, who scorned all men, and scorned my goats,
My shepherd's flute, my shaggy beard and eyebrows,
And thought the gods cared nothing for anything human,
That she should be the bride of such as him!
        My flute, begin to play Maenalus' song.
I saw you, when you were a little child.
Your mother was with you. I led you to the place
In our garden where there was the apple tree,
With dewy apples growing on the boughs.
I was just going on twelve, just tall enough

To reach up to the branches to pick the apples.
I saw, I saw, and I was lost forever.
       My flute, begin to play Maenalus' song.
I know what Love is. He was born on the rocks
Of Tmaros or of Rhodope or else
Far in the Garamantian Desert. Love
Is not of our **blood** and he is not of our kind.
       My flute, begin to play Maenalus' song.
Love taught a mother how to stain her hands
With the blood of her children. Tell me, Mother, which
Of the two of you was the crueler **one**? Which one
Of **the** two, was it, Mother, cruel Love, or you?
       My flute, begin to play Maenalus' song.
Let wolves run away from sheep, let **golden apples**
Suddenly be the fruit of mighty oaks,
Narcissus bloom **on the boughs** of adder trees,
And amber ooze from **the bark** of tamarisks;
Let owls complete with swans, and Tityrus
Compete with Orpheus—an Orpheus of the woods,
Let Tityrus be Arion among the dolphins.
       My flute, begin to play Maenalus' song.
Farewell to woods, let **all** be ocean now.
Headlong I'll **fall** to my death **from this** high cliff.
My song be my last offering to you.
       *Thus ends, my flute, the **song** of Maenalus."*

A GREAT MANY SIGNS OF A VERY BITTER COLD TO COME

And how I measured them, how I watched the clouds
in the morning, watched the soot in the hearth for sparks.
Wolves more fierce. The air like thorns in my eyes.
Nails springing from the walls. How I hoped I was wrong,
and knew I wasn't. My feet hard as bone.
The stones breaking beneath the skin of the field.
The wild animals trying to get in.

ABSOLUTE ZERO

The cold kissed the blossoms into blue

at my door. *I've ridden all night*, it said, *to find you, who*

*left me for dead—*said

come all this way to show you

my place in your bed. Lead

sky, lead hand, lead tongue wrung

to nothing, to absolute zero, narrow

in the mouth. *Thought you could leave me—see*

how wrong you were. I saw how all night long, song

blew its snow past the window. *Lo,*

it said, *be held, hold*

me in your bed. How I did. How cold called

my name, and how I answered, word-

less: *yes.*

THE SNOW RECKONER

In every direction, *beckon*

shivers apart and scatters into flakes of snow, so

many that Archimedes could have penned another *Reckoner*.

But these grains are not sand—are made to undo

themselves: filling, unfilling,

then filling the universe again before they're

frozen in

a formula. I know that there are

more flakes in this field than cells in my body,

that this field is a body that could swallow me whole—cell

after cell settling into crystals, needles,

rosettes of bloodless ice.

Pointless to keep counting, then, when

a body and a field are one horizon.

DIAMOND DUST

My eyes burn like meteors against this field, which is a sky,

which is a tundra

of sundogs and solar wind, which stitch

my sight with froth.

The movement of the ocean: forgotten.

In its place: a blue tongue rolling down the nave of

my brain, licking the idea

of *ocean* into dry ice, into a halo of diamond dust. Coldest

hallucination, particulate sheen, shun

my eye.

Shut it

inside the oyster of your sky. Let me be

your grit, your snowy ache. Bed me like a pearl. Lay me

in the field of your nacre.

MELTWATER

My eyelids flicker and burn, then open

onto dreams that are filled with a strange new glow,

even though snow

has never fallen harder. When the sunrise tries

to woo me with its quartz-cold tongue, I let it—

I press my lip to the window to

feel its pulse like a betrothal on my mouth. When I say

soften me into a stream, load my veins with sleet, it

does, and I run down-

hill into a hollow

and become lake, lakebed, bed-

rock numb beneath the water table. No glow

down here, just palest

night—its eyes like rapture's mirrors.

MAELSTROM

There is less *yes*

than darkness here, more

ebb than swell of light. Night

after night, I dream of pendulums frozen mid-swing, swung

toward the North, and wake in a maelstrom of my own frozen

breath. Beneath

its haze, my eyes glaze

over. I am being ground down into the ocean bed, head

heavy as a rock, and somewhere down-current, am being found, blind

with silt, fish in my throat. I wake again to black windows, to my frost-broken reflection.

Hours until morning. Hours since I got into bed. *A land of darkness, as*

darkness itself, where the light is as

darkness, on whose meadows

the cold kisses the blossoms into blue.

FISSURE

A nightmare ruptures my eye

and I stumble into awareness as

onto a dim staircase of reasons why I

cannot sleep at night.

Outside, the road winks with ice, malice

soft as the smell of gas—easy, sly:

Let's go for a ride. Centuries ago, in polar winter,

tribes would race their horses across snow-packed chasms, on stone-

hard rivers. Fissures

sometimes swallowed them whole, horse and rider together.

Say they

broke in the fall, fell

into lore. Or did they wake—rider and ridden open-

eyed, a meteor across the green field of the sky?

WINTER FIELD

It's easy to get lost out here, on fields of nacre your

eye can't fasten on.

The map is inconclusive, sieve-

like: directions and distances vanish into one sheen

as if they were never there.

Thin air. Or else they multiply

like flakes of snow. How long can a body be

exposed to cold before it dies? For the record, Lord,

I don't want to know. Why test your creature?

Why press your iron weather to my cheek, meek

already, ready

to rest on winter's sheet? Spare me from experiment. Reorient

my body's compass

and from every direction, beckon.

PARALLAX

My body and this field have become a single horizon, frozen

beneath the white of Janus' *I*'s:

Castor and Pollux, their arms entwined, twinned

in the sky's face,

which presses my own into a deeper winter,

into a cold whiter than moon

on snow, sharper than its rind pinned

overhead. I half know a thaw is coming, half know it will never come. Gem-

eyed, the twins jump from left to right when I wink. Fickle as ice,

as space,

one whispers, *Give it time.* The other whispers, *Give it up.* In one

translation of the stars, summer's

constellations are being born. Their burn-

ing eyelids flicker. Then open.

SIRIUS

Heat unrolls its tongue across us like paint.
Dense as the breath of a panting hound,

it solders us chest to chest until we are a pair
of lungs, one breastbone between us.

We take turns breathing. You gasp in fields of sawgrass
and asters. I gasp in riverbeds and the grassy beds of deer.

We breathe so hard that our sight dies in patches—
a star shape dies from my left eye, a pyramid from your right.

Slowly this bites the fields into constellations
whose myths are bad-starred and blighted as we are.

There is The Stray Dog, there The Broken-Winged Bird,
The Torn Sail. They crumble into our mouths like dirt.

We touch each other and feel the mange, the feathers,
the sailcloth parting beneath our fingers.

We cannot see what darker matter
is trying to emerge.

HELIOSPHERE

Un-compassed, our *here*
was an everywhere, was an atom blown open
into an infinite net
with us at its center.
                        For
years the sun was our bellwether,
then it was sequences
of clouds, then a sparrow's wing arrowing
east across a field, propelled
toward infinity without ever landing.
                             We were lost, cast
like chaff into an undefined wind.
We spun through lozenges of farmland, spellbound
and blur-eyed as the grass rose
like a wall before our hands again and again, margin-
less.
    We spun and our spinning was a ring gathering
our blood into our hands until our *everywhere*
tightened into a tiny, incalculable frontier.
                             Then adrift, aloft,
a molecule of the wind's howl; an owl's afterfeather landing along-
side a wet field of foals; shells
crumbling into their surrounding seas—
                           please,
I said with my mouth to the earth, *not yet.*

But the dirt was ice
on my face. From the sudden snow I felt no echo.

TERMINATION SHOCK

Somewhere behind us is something like a sun.
We have stopped riding our fevers and they have stopped
       running, have broken through some tall fence
       and are grazing on the other side.
We are sweating, still expecting the sun to appear
       and burn our faces with its face.
As if anything could ever love us that bluntly again.

But we can't stop reaching: you dig a deep ditch
       and we lie in it to see all the angles of the sky.
I chop down an entire hill, un-root
       a nest of field mice and kneel by its latent heat,
       put my cheek to the tiny wheat-filled hollows.

Cooling. Everything we touch.
Our beds are snow, our legs are river water.
A wind is blowing from somewhere across the meadow,
       carrying a new sound, a slowing, a deepening pitch.
Our blood beats with it until there is no blood left.
The shock entered me like it was coming home.

BLACK COMETS

Night falls on our faces and stays down.

The world is a bolt of black cloth
that something is tearing into pieces.

We can hear the river running rockier
for an instant before draining away.

We can hear the waterfall falling into deeper space.

The pieces fall invisibly past us
but we have learned to catch their echoes

like sonar as they pass. There went
a slice of prairie, there a branch,

a tuft of birch leaves, a glance of sky that leaves
a trail of black prisms in your eye,

there went half a burning meadowlark.
Its one wing brushes fire into my hair.

With our crow voices we call like pulsars
to each other. We can feel the black fireflies

weaving wildly through the air as if trying
to tie it back together.

THAW

During the first night of the thaw, the snow ebbed
to reveal damp fields of corn husks.
                                    I folded them into flowers,
made a simple doll the weight of a bird.

In the darkness, you saw none of this—you,
who also are dead, who have been dead so long
your voice has become birdsong whenever I try to hear it in my head,
which I often do, often at night, when there usually are no birds.

This has distorted my sense of time. The bird seems to whistle minutes,
its syrinx a timepiece made of bone.
                                    I no longer need clocks,
have stopped winding them.
                        The house is full of dead clocks
and my head is full of birds and my skull has become a columbary,

which is why, on the night the thaw started, I didn't hear
the fields loosening. The lapwings in my head warped around the sound
of snapping roots and running water.
                                    What woke me up was the sudden heat.
I went outside and watched a snowbank sink in fast motion.
It made a chirping sound, like a tape being rewound.
                                    I made
the doll, the flowers. The snowbank chirped like a wounded bird,
which sounds like any other bird.

HAUNT

My future ghost has been growing uneasy. It has been growing
its hay inside me forever, a soft scarecrow with its back
to the setting sun. Now it feels pulled across my body's field as if
by some magnet. When two ghosts touch, their nexus is a canceling-out,
a lukewarm vanishing. When you touch the dying parts of me,
I feel them go numb, as if being prepared for amputation.
I have learned to sleep with my back to the wall, my eyes hugely open,
two pale eggs. I count my breaths for protection. I count the parts of me
that are left. A ghost is a zero multiplying everything by itself,
and I am too empty to repel that tenderness.

Thus Damon's song. Pierian maidens, come,
Help me to tell how Alphesiboeus replied.

ALPHESIBOEUS

"Bring water, and bring **the** ribbons of **softest wool**
To wind around the altar, and light the fire
Of aromatic woods and frankincense
To make the incense smoke, and I will with
Such magic strive to change my lover's mind.
All that is needful now is a charm to sing.

       Bring Daphnis home, bring Daphnis home, my charms.
Charms **can** entice the moon down out of the sky;
Ulysses' men were changed by Circe's charms;
Charms can cause the snake in the field to burst.

       Bring Daphnis home, bring Daphnis home, my charms.
I **weave** the threads around your image thrice,
Three-colored threads, and carry the image thrice
Around the altar, for the god loves threes.

       Bring Daphnis home, bring Daphnis home, my charms.
Weave, Amaryllis, we**a**ve, three threads around,
And make three times three-colored knots, and say
'With these three threads I weave the **chain**s of love.'

       Bring Daphnis home, bring Daphnis home, my charms.
As in one fire this image made **of** clay
Grows hard and this of wax grows soft, so may
The heart of Daphnis melt for love of me.
Cast meal about, light bitumen **pitch and burn**
The crackling laurel boughs: Daphnis burns **me**:
This in the laurel fire may Daphnis melt.

       Bring Daphnis home, bring Daphnis home, my charms.
May he be seized by such desire as that
Of a **lovesick** heifer longing for her bull,
Who weary and lost from following where he went
Lies down in the grass that grows beside the stream
That through the deep woods flows; weary and lost,

Forgetful of her home far **in**to the night;
May he be seized by such desire as hers,
And I not care at all to be the cure.
    Bring Daphnis home, bring Daphnis home, my charms.
These garments he, perfidious, left as pledges;
Now I comm**it** them, earth, to you before
The threshold of my house; these garments are
The pledges that my Daphnis belongs to me.

GIVEN

A point is that which has no part
Euclid

A given
is always

a point
of departure,

a puncture,
origin of

a wound,
some newness.

For example,
this given:

that points
are partless,

when really
they're couple-

numbered, binary;
the way,

no matter
how fast

it flies,
a bluebird's

blue can
never outstrip

its *bird,*
or *butter*

drain from
its *cup,*

rattle shed
its *snake.*

What would
it do,

that bird—
unblue, unselved,

blanched on
winter's branch,

absent against
its white?

Without you,
I'm only

the idea
of flight.

NULL

If gravity is a yield.

Is the falling into
of a field.

If of sunflowers.

If I am pulled
into their orbits
with heavy-headed hunger,
with urge.

If curvature.

If a million mirrors
mirror the suns
I bury myself among.

If I'm uprooted
and re-flung
toward the sun,
face-first.

If *perihelion.*

If my faith
to the field
is uncertain
as a hawk's flight
from a lureless glove.

If so, let me

flutter between
these two surfaces
of sun
in an endless
catch and fall.

Let my face burn,
bereaving,
wherever I turn.

GRAVITY WELL

Mid-June,
mid-nowhere,
the sun mid-
somersault,
the weather
wool-heavy.
A lungful
of it weighs
like water,
a field of it
bends corn-
stalks toward
the earth's
center. If I
enter this field,
the black soil
will dilate
beneath
my feet,
root systems
draining
into its pupil
like light.
Even if I
move now,
it's already
too late.
I met
the bottom
of this well
years ago.
And if I

turn to wave
at someone
walking past
the field,
she will see
what she
always sees:
a person
the color
of a sunset
waving
what looks
like a flag.

SOLSTICE

Snowflakes fall on the white river. Snowflakes the size of hawks
land in the trees. I stand on the river's shoulder, which has become
the bottom of the ocean. My arms are two methane lakes, my hands
opening and closing like mussels at their edges. Deep-sea isopods,
white from no light, fall around me in mountains. When hauled
to the surface, they will shiver into hills of slush.

But the snowflakes aren't melting. At midday the river is a gasp
banked by hours of darkness. The snow is sharp with pressure.
There is no room for shivering. I stare until the river fills with light.
In your absence, my heart has grown so large, so white.

HUNT

These new nights are full of blind country where your scent curls
into the knots of trees, clings to the undersides of leaves like chrysalides.
Your ghost has gone to ground, has denned itself somewhere dark
and unhoundable. The pain is ultraviolet. Beneath its rays
my heart mutates into a hawk, its eyes locked on the pack of hounds
that have become my guts. My body bays and screeches, plunging
into dream thickets, too foolish to turn tail and wake up.
Each day dawns blank beneath a neutral, unforgiveable sun.

Bring Daphnis home, bring Daphnis home, my charms.
Moeris gave me these herbs and poison plants
That come from Pontus, where they grow aplenty.
How often **I have seen** how by their aid
He turned into **a wolf loping away**
Into the woods, and I **have seen him** use them
To **call up ghosts** out of their graves, or cause
The seeds one farmer just put down in his field
To fly away at night to grow in another's.
Bring Daphnis home, bring Daphnis home, my charms.
Now, Amaryllis, take the embers out
And carry them to a stream, and turn around,
And throw them over your shoulder into the stream,
And don't look back. **Thus** will I win back Daphnis,
Who doesn't know what gods and charms can do.
Bring Daphnis home, bring Daphnis home, my charms.
O see! before **they**'re carried out the ashes
Suddenly, of their own accord, **burst forth,**
And the altar burns once more **with quivering** flames.
Let this be good.—I think it may be good.
The dog is **bark**ing down by the front gate.
Can I believe it, or is it that lovers dream?
Cease now, my charms, my Daphnis has come home!

DOVER IN NOVEMBER

I.

Tonight

is a cold cliff I lean over. Tonight is a fair

blank face. Think of the way light

lusters an edge of something, sharpens a stand

of poplars. Think of the way an animal faces the baying

hound, the night air

warming around the hound's tongue, the rain spraying

surrender into the animal's fur. Each year, the land

crushes new parts of itself into the water. It dreams of the sea's roar,

of the sea's mouth, of the fling

of itself down the sea's throat. It dreams that each strand

of seagrass began in a dry meadow and wonders whether it can begin

there again if it closes its eyes. I cannot bring

this night into focus. I cannot bring myself in.

II.

In a late summer garden, years ago,

I watched as a thrush brought

a snail down against a rock until its shell broke. The thrush's song was a low

tremolo as it dismantled the snail's softness and we—

I and my two eyes watching—thought

is this what it's like to be a pebble in the mouth of the sea?

III.

Daybreak: the sky is faith-

white, closed as a cockle shell from cloud-shore

to cloud-shore. The horizon is a furled

sound that loosens with light until, at noon, all I hear

is the glare, the waves' roar

like a razor blade under my tongue until dusk, when the water's breath

blurs even the whelk's spires. Dear

self: I lied about the cliff. I am already falling through one world

IV.

and into the other. There is something halfway true

in this. There is no other world, but I have already fallen into it, and it seems

clearer. Between my dreams

of the panting hound, of the shell-less snail—a new

dream: light

on a meadow. Vast heat. A pain

white and soft as milk, and plain

as a blade of grass, as a bird's flight

drawn against a cloudless night.

ANSWER

after May Swenson

I will mount
a bright horse.

I will know what it is
to shift and quicken.

I will hound ahead
without *with* or roof.

Where I will go
(eager door, cloud-thicket, *in*),
my hide will ride.

Body my fallen sky,
my treasure-dog,

be good when dead.
Hunt without danger or sleep.

Body, when you are all
I can do, how I will lie.

How I will house the wind
in my eye.

VIRGIL

The muse of the shepherd Alphesiboeus and Damon,
At whose contending songs the very cattle
Were **spellbound in the field,** forgetting to graze—
The lynx was **spellbound** too, hearing the music—
And the rivers, spellbound, stood still listening—
I sing the Muse of Damon and Alphesiboeus.
Whether it be that you are passing by
The great rocks **at the mouth of the river** Timavus
Or sailing homeward along the Illyrian coast,
I long for the day when I shall be able to sing
In celebration of your victories,
And celebrate to all the **world** as well
Your Sophoclean music. These songs of mine,
In my beginning, are for you; and **when**
I come to the end, it shall be in your service.
Accept these songs written at your command;
May these few **i**vy leaves **be among your** laurels.

LULLABY

The loon's eye is a carmine moon.

Is a Mars. Stirs

in its orbit as the wind stirs the lake's loose face

into haloes whose

arcs swell against each other until they disappear or

are blown into new diagrams, battle plans, lessons

for a war that cannot

reach us here, in this pocket of pine forest I tuck you into.

Hush. Thrush

and snail, moth and bat, are reconciled, held

in the same dark mouth.
                         When you ask for a story, I

hum the names of lunar seas—*Nubium, Imbrium*

Vaporum, Crisium—

which are not seas, whose

water is a dark silt, basalt

shallows empty enough to look like

a face.

When you ask for a song, I sing about the hole in the bottom of the sea,

a lesson in

microscopy, in vertigo. *O*

little eye, little eye, there's always a further layer,

an infinite splitting, a tunneling. Sung,

this is

just soft enough to sleep by.

The loon's eye gleams and drifts on the lake like

a broken beacon

above a slow drain. Like a body orbiting a black hole. Wool

being drawn from a cloud to a thread to the pupil of a needle's eye.

Hush-a-bye,

hush-a-bye, I

didn't mean to make you cry. The lake is a lake, the loon a loon, the eye

was only ever an eye.

A red-throated

morning yawns in the sky.

Now give me the goat and the carved cup. Let me milk her
And **drink** to **the** Muses.
                              Muses, goodbye, but only
For the moment! In time I shall sing you a sweeter **song**

GOATHERD

Then, Thyrsis, you must **stop your mouth with sweetness,**
Eat only **honeycomb and** the best dried figs,
Since, even as it is, you out-sing the **cicada.**
Here is the cup. Smell the scented wood, so fresh
You would think it had been dipped at **the well** of the Hours.
Cissaetha!
              Yours for milking!
                                Gently, my goats,
Down! or you'll have the billy goat force you **down.**

PRAYER

All shall be well,   and all shall be well,

and all wells shall yield   their missing

children,   and all manner of children

shall feel their bedroom walls   with cold

hands   still smelling of well water,

and all men shall cover their wells,

and how could they fail, and how could

we all,   and if we call from the bottom

of a well, who shall hear, and what shall

haul us out   but our own hands,   and when

shells fall   from the bowl of the sky,

shall they fall into the hollows   of our hands,

shall our hands explode   into holes, shall

our bodies crumple   like the hulls of ships,

and when the well cover closes   over us

and we have not called out,   shall we still

call out in the dark,   shall we feel the walls

with our hands? Somewhere, summer turns

to fall.   Across the hills, the sun pulls

its small light down.

NOTES

"A Great Many Signs of a Very Bitter Cold to Come" & "On Making One's Passage in the Dark": These titles refer to sections of Olaus Magnus' *A Description of the Northern Peoples* (1555).

"Maelstrom": The italicized lines are taken from The Book of Job 10:22 (KJV).

"Dover in November": This poem preserves the last words of each line of Matthew Arnold's "Dover Beach."

"Answer": This poem is a rearrangement of the words of May Swenson's "Question."

"[I am spellbound in the field]," "[I have seen a wolf]," "[The dew is an O]," and "[Thus the softest wool]" are erasures of Virgil's *Eclogue VIII* from *The Eclogues of Virgil* translated by David Ferry. Copyright © 1999 by David Ferry. Reprinted by permission of Farrar, Straus and Giroux.

"[your touch is a sweetness]," "[grief is not a great river]," and "[Now drink the song]" are erasures of Theocritus' *Idyll 1* from *The Idylls of Theocritus* translated by Robert Wells. Copyright © 1988 by Robert Wells. Reprinted by permission of Carcanet Press Limited.

ACKNOWLEDGMENTS

Grateful acknowledgement is made to the editors of the following journals where these poems, sometimes in earlier versions and under different titles, first appeared:

32 Poems: "Solstice," "Fallow," "The Valley"

Bateau: "The Next World," "Nativity, Redshift," "Redmouth"

Birdfeast: "Answer"

The Blueshift Journal: "Elegy Where My Sorrow Appears as an Undiscovered Land," "Thaw"

The Boiler: "My Life as a Nightjar," "Sirius"

The Cincinnati Review: "Nocturne"

The Collapsar: "Termination Shock"

Connotation Press: "Requiem," "On Making One's Passage in the Dark," "Instar"

Handsome: "Breach"

The Kenyon Review Online: "Given"

LEVELER: "Black Comets"

Literary Matters: "[The dew is an O]," "[Thus the softest wool]," "[I have seen a wolf]," "[I am spellbound in the field]"

The Louisville Review: "Haunt"

Memorious: "Beast & Master," "Preserve," "A Great Many Signs of a Very Bitter Cold to Come"

Parcel: "Hunt"

The Paris-American: "Dehiscence"

Sugared Water: "Gravity Well"

Third Coast: "Prayer"

Tinderbox Poetry Journal: "Diamond Dust," "Dover in November," "Null"

Unsplendid: "Absolute Zero," "The Snow Reckoner," "Winter Field," "Meltwater," "Fissure," "Parallax"

Waxwing: "Children Arrive in the Land I Thought I Was Alone In," "Heliosphere," "Lullaby"

West Branch: "[your touch is a sweetness]," "[grief is not a great river]," "[Now drink the song]"

Thanks to Katharine Coles, Michael Lavers, and Jacqueline Osherow for their guidance, and to the editorial team at Tinderbox Editions for riding shotgun with me.

Endless gratitude to Laura Bylenok, Sara Eliza Johnson, Daniel Lupton, and Susannah Nevison, who know this book almost better than I do.

Claire Wahmanholm is the author of *Night Vision*, winner of the 2017 New Michigan Press/ DIAGRAM chapbook competition, and *Wilder*, winner of the 2018 Lindquist & Vennum Prize for Poetry. Her poems have appeared in *Grist*, *RHINO*, *32 Poems*, *West Branch*, *The Southeast Review*, *The Los Angeles Review*, *The Paris-American*, *Bomb Cyclone*, *Fairy Tale Review*, *New Poetry from the Midwest 2017*, *PANK*, and *Bennington Review*. She lives and teaches in the Twin Cities.